Animal World

Alligators

Donna Bailey and Christine Butterworth

STECK-VAUGHN
LIBRARY
A Division of Steck-Vaughn Company

Look at this alligator floating
under the water.
It looks like a floating log!

2

An alligator can lie just under
the water for hours.
It is waiting to catch a fish.
It grabs the fish in its strong jaws.

This alligator has climbed
onto the riverbank to catch a turtle.
Alligators eat small birds and
snakes, as well as fish and turtles.

Alligators spend most of their day
lying in the sun on muddy riverbanks.
Alligators are cold-blooded animals.
They need the heat of the sun
to keep warm.

As winter comes and the days
get cooler, the alligator digs
a long burrow in the muddy riverbank.
Its sharp claws help it dig.
It will sleep in the burrow all winter.

When the alligator wakes up in
the spring, it is very hungry.
It slithers down to the river
to find food.

Alligators mate in the spring.

The males roar in the night to call the females.

When two males meet, they fight.

They bite each other with their sharp teeth.

The strongest male will mate with the female.

8

After the alligators mate in the water,
the female swims back to the riverbank.
She makes a nest from leaves, plants, and
mud.
It is almost three feet high.

The female uses her back feet to dig
a hole in the top of the pile.
She lays up to 70 eggs in the hole.
She covers them with wet leaves and mud.
The eggs are warmed by the hot sun.

The female stays near the nest and
watches it.
She guards her nest for two months.
She drives off any animals that
try to eat the eggs.

One day, the mother hears tiny croaks
from inside the nest.
The baby alligators are hatching!

The mother digs into the nest
to help her babies get out.

The mother takes the baby alligators
to a safe place near the water.
She carries them in her mouth
or on her head.
She takes care of the babies for one year.

14

The young alligators grow fast.
They call their mother when
there is danger.
Many baby alligators are eaten by fish,
birds, or other alligators.

Alligators can live to be 50 years old.
But people have killed many alligators.
At one time, people hunted alligators for
their skins.

Farmers drained the swamps where the alligators lived.

Without their homes, many alligators died.

Now, some alligators live on alligator farms.

When the baby alligators are big enough, they are set free in the wild.

This is a Chinese alligator.

It is only about five feet long.

There are not many left in the world,

but you may see one in a zoo.

This alligator lives in the lakes, swamps, and slow-moving streams of Florida. An adult alligator often grows to about 13 feet long.

Crocodiles and alligators often hunt
and fight in the water.
They must keep water out of their throat.
When they open their mouth, a special flap
at the back of their throat keeps water out.

Crocodiles and alligators can also grow
new teeth in the place of the ones they lose.
This crocodile has just caught a fish.
Look at its sharp teeth!

Crocodiles are not the same as alligators.
An alligator has a broad snout, but
a crocodile's snout is much narrower.
When a crocodile shuts its mouth,
you can still see many of its teeth.

Nile crocodiles often live together in
groups in the lakes and rivers of Africa.
They like to lie on muddy riverbanks.
Little birds hop inside their open mouths
to peck the dirt off their teeth!

A group of crocodiles may hunt together
to kill a big animal, like a deer or a hippo.
When the deer comes to drink, a crocodile
grabs it and pulls it under water to drown it.

This crocodile is waiting for its prey.
It has swallowed stones to make its body
heavier so that it will stay under water.
Only the top of its head shows above
the water.

This crocodile has found a deer
lying on its side near the river.
The crocodile carefully goes up to the deer
to see if it's still alive.

26

The crocodile walks around the deer.
It is lucky.
The deer is dead, so the crocodile
can drag it back to the river.

The crocodile stores the body of
the deer under water.
When the deer flesh becomes soft,
the crocodile can tear off pieces to eat.

These giant estuarine crocodiles live
in salt water around the coasts of
Asia and Australia.
They are very fierce and can grow up
to 30 feet long.

This gavial lives in the rivers of India.

Gavials are much like crocodiles.

You can tell a gavial by its long, narrow snout.

30

Gavials swish their snouts through the water to trap fish in their sharp teeth.

Gavials have become rare.
Like crocodiles and alligators,
they were killed for their skins.
These young gavials live on
a special farm so they won't become extinct.

32

Index

Reading Consultant: Diana Bentley
Editorial Consultant: Donna Bailey
Executive Editor: Elizabeth Strauss
Project Editor: Becky Ward

Picture research by Jennifer Garratt
Designed by Richard Garratt Design

Photographs
Cover: Bruce Coleman (M. Stone)
Ardea: 28 (Richard Walker)
Bruce Coleman: 2,16 (Dr. Eckart Pott), 3 (Bruce Coleman), 5,18 (Norman Owen Tomalin), 6 (Leonard Lee Rue III), 9,12, 13,14 (Jeff Simon), 10,11 (James Simon), 15 (Jeff Foott), 22 (Goetz D. Plage), 23 (Alan Root), 24,26,27 (Gunter Ziesler), 25 (Lee Lyon), 31, 32 (Mike Price)
OSF Picture Library: title page, 4,19 (Stan Osolinski), 7 (Jack Dermid), 8,20 (E. Robinson), 17 (Terry Heathcote), 21 (Maurice Tibbles), 29 (Mickey Gibson), 30 (Z. Leszcynski)

Library of Congress Cataloging-in-Publication Data: Butterworth, Christine. Alligators / Christine Butterworth and Donna Bailey. p. cm.—(Animal world) Includes index. SUMMARY: Explores the world of alligators, croco-diles, and their rare relative the gavial, describing their physical characteristics, habitat, and behavior. ISBN 0-8114-2639-4 1. Alligators—Juvenile literature. [1. Alligators. 2. Crocodiles.] I. Bailey, Donna. II. Title. III. Series: Animal world (Austin, Tex.) QL666.C925B88 1990 597.98—dc20 90-9927 CIP AC

ISBN 0-8114-2639-4
Copyright 1991 Steck-Vaughn Company
Original copyright Heinemann Children's Reference 1991

2 3 4 5 6 7 8 9 0 LB 96 95 94 93 92 91